M/V Columbia Star 2003

Sailing the Great Lakes

Life on the Iron Ore Freighters

Timothy Spears

M/V Columbia Star 2003

Sailing the Great Lakes

Life on the Iron Ore Freighters

By

Timothy Spears
Copyright 2019 Timothy Spears LLC

About the author:

Timothy sailed in the Merchant Marines on the Great Lakes for about 10 years in the 1970's.
He worked in the engine room on all the ships he sailed on.
He worked at the U.S. Coast Guard Marine Safety Office in Toledo Ohio for eight years.
Prior to working at the Coast Guard, he drove a tractor-trailer over the road for 20 years.

I always knew ever since I was a young boy of 11 years old that someday I would sail on a ship. Since my father was a sailor and an over the road truck driver, I guess I was a chip off the old block.

I remember riding out to the docks in the car with my father and watching the ships come into the Port of Toledo and unloading their cargo.

As I sat there in the car with my dad, and he explained to me what the men up on the ship were doing, I watched them, and thought to myself "that has got to be the coolest job in the world".

That was the very moment that I decided someday I was going to sail on a ship just like those guys I was watching. As soon as I turned 18 years old, I went down to the Coast Guard office in Toledo an applied for my merchant marine credential. I shipped out within a month from the Lake Carrier's hall with the next available job that came up.

As luck would have it, the job happened to be an engine room job which I would prefer over the galley or deck jobs. That was the beginning of my 10-year career sailing in the engine room.

All photos were taken by the author unless otherwise noted.
All text was written by author unless noted otherwise.

Note to Amazon;

Text is available under the Creative Commons Attribution-ShareAlike License; additional terms may apply. By using this site, you agree to the Terms of Use and Privacy Policy. Wikipedia® is a registered trademark of the Wikimedia Foundation, Inc., a non-profit organization.

(Photo by NASA)

Lake Superior has an area of 31700 square miles, Lake Superior has a length of 349.8 Miles. Lake Superior has a depth of 1332 ft. according to Wikipedia there is enough water in Lake Superior to cover the entire landmass of North and South America to a depth of 30cm (12 inches), the shoreline of the leg stretches 2726 miles.

The Great Lakes were formed nearly 20,000 years ago when the earth's climate warmed and the last glacial Continental ice sheet retreated, the glacier up to 2 miles thick, was so heavy and powerful it gouged out the Earth's surface to create the lake basins.

The Great Lakes are a series of interconnected freshwater lakes in the upper mid-east region of North America on the Canada-United States border.

U.S.-flagged ships moved over 83 million tons of cargo in 2016 with iron ore for steel production being the primary cargo at over 44 million tons.

The Great Lakes Waterway (GLW) is a system of natural channels and canals which enable navigation between the North American Great Lakes. Though all of the lakes are naturally connected as a chain, water travel between the lakes was impeded for centuries by obstacles such as Niagara Falls and the rapids of the St. Mary's River.

Its principal civil engineering works are the Welland Canal between Lakes Ontario and Erie, and the huge Soo Locks between Huron and Superior. Dredged channels were constructed in the St. Mary's River, the Detroit River, Lake St. Clair and the St. Clair River between Huron and Erie. Usually, one or more U.S. Coast Guard icebreakers help keep the water passage open for part of the fall and early winter, although shipping usually ceases for two to three months thereafter.

The St. Lawrence Seaway allows navigable shipping from the GLW to the Atlantic Ocean, while the Illinois Waterway extends commercial shipping to the Mississippi River and the Gulf of Mexico. The Great Lakes Waterway is co-administered by the governments of Canada and the United States of America.

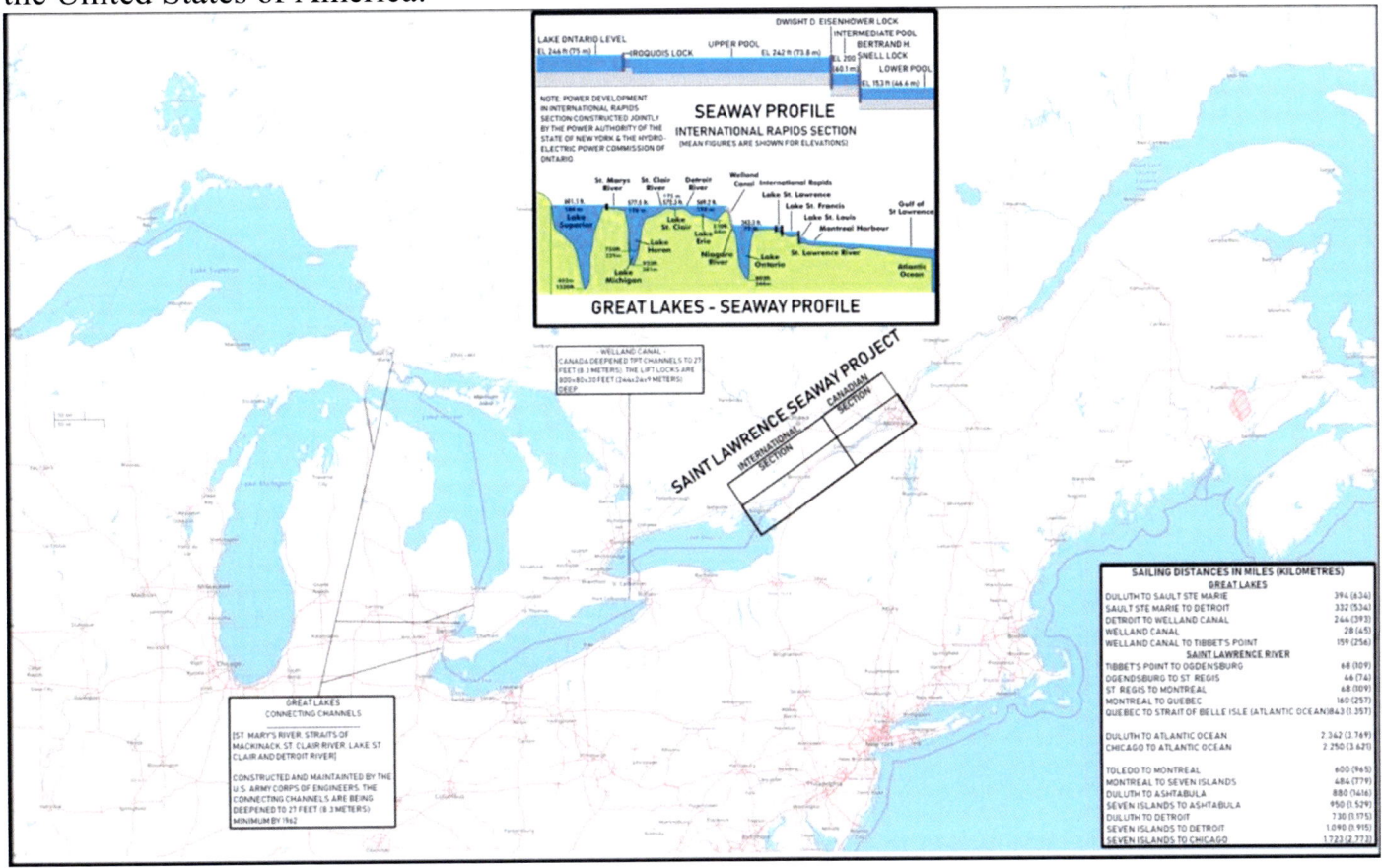

(source Wikipedia)

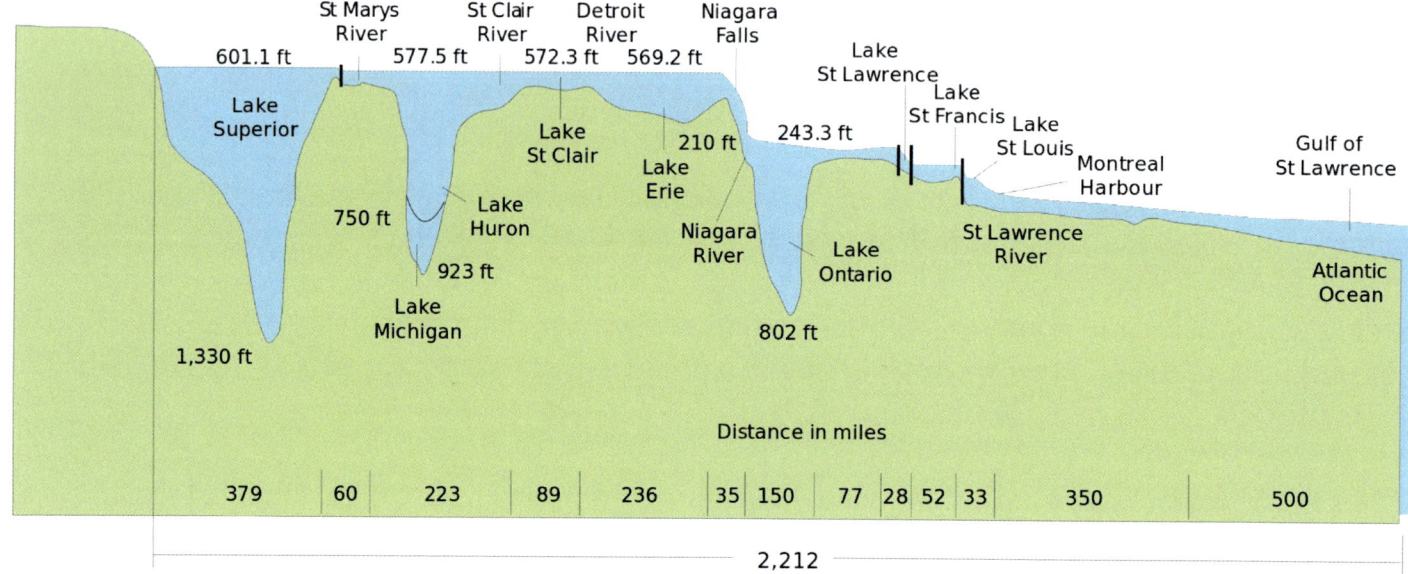
(source Wikipedia)

Soo Locks - (photo U.S. Army Corp of Engineers)

The waterway allows passage from the Atlantic Ocean to the inland port of Duluth on Lake Superior, a distance of 2,340 miles, and to Chicago, on Lake Michigan, at 2,250 miles.

Together with the Saint Lawrence Seaway, the Waterway allows both ocean-going vessels and the ore, grain and coal-bearing lake freighters to travel from the system's saltwater outlet to its far interior. The Waterway has larger locks and deeper drafts than the lower Seaway, limiting large freighters to the four lakes upstream of the Welland Canal and Lake Ontario and similarly restricting passage beyond Saint Lambert, Quebec by larger ocean vessels. The two waterways are often jointly and simply referred to as the "St. Lawrence Seaway", since the Great Lakes, together with the St. Lawrence River, comprise a single navigable body of freshwater linking the Atlantic Ocean to the continental interior of the United States.

Shipping channels separate upbound traffic from down-bound traffic. The upbound direction is away from the St. Lawrence River (westerly or northerly except in Lake Michigan where upbound is southerly). Channels are marked with navigation buoys in constricted areas and pilots are required on foreign boats. Recreational boats can use or cross the ship channels, but the large boats, with limited maneuverability, have right of way.

Lake freighters, or Lakers, are bulk carrier vessels that ply the Great Lakes of North America.

These vessels are traditionally called boats, although classified as ships.
Since the late 19th century, Lakers carry bulk cargoes of materials such as limestone, iron ore, grain, coal, or salt from the mines and fields of the upper Great Lakes to the populous industrial areas down the lakes. The 63 commercial ports handled 173 million tons of cargo in 2006. Because of winter ice on the lakes, the navigation season is not usually year-round. The Soo Locks and Welland Canal close from mid-January to late March, when most boats are laid up for maintenance. Crewmembers spend these months ashore.

Depending on their application, Lakers may also be referred to by their type, such as ore boats (primarily for iron ore), straight deckers (no self-unloading gear), bulkers (carry bulk cargo), stern enders (all cabins aft), self-unloaders (with self-unloading gear), longboats (for their slender appearance), or lake boats, among others.

In the mid-20th century, 300 Lakers worked the Lakes, but by the early 21st century there were fewer than 140 active Lakers. The SS Edmund Fitzgerald, which sank in 1975, became widely known as the most recent and largest major vessel to be wrecked on the Great Lakes.

Sault Ste Marie Michigan

The Soo Locks (sometimes spelled Sault Locks but pronounced "soo") are a set of parallel locks, operated and maintained by the U.S. Army Corps of Engineers, Detroit District, which enable ships to travel between Lake Superior and the lower Great Lakes. Built: 1855 (photo Army Corp of Engineers) Picture looking north, Canada on the right.

The St. Lawrence Seaway

The Saint Lawrence Seaway (French: la Voie Maritime du Saint-Laurent) is a system of locks, canals, and channels in Canada and the United States that permits oceangoing vessels to travel from the Atlantic Ocean to the Great Lakes of North America, as far inland as the western end of Lake Superior. The seaway is named for the Saint Lawrence River, which flows from Lake Ontario to the Atlantic Ocean. Legally, the seaway extends from Montreal, Quebec, to Lake Erie and includes the Welland Canal. (Source Wikipedia)

(Photo Wikipedia)

The Eisenhower Locks in Massena, New York.
(Photo Wikipedia)

The Saint Lawrence River portion of the seaway is not a continuous canal; rather, it consists of several stretches of navigable channels within the river, a number of locks, and canals along the banks of the Saint Lawrence River to bypass several rapids and dams. A number of the locks are managed by the St. Lawrence Seaway Management Corporation in Canada, and others in the United States by the Saint Lawrence Seaway Development Corporation; the two bodies together advertise the seaway as part of "Highway H2O". The section of the river from Montreal to the Atlantic is under Canadian jurisdiction, regulated by the offices of Transport Canada in the Port of Quebec.

A self-unloading Ship opens gates in the cargo hold to allow cargo to drop onto the conveyor belt and sent up to the unloading boom where it is dumped on the shore. This method can work with coal, iron ore and limestone.

(SS J. Burton Ayers at Detroit Edison plant, Detroit River, Ambassador bridge in background)

Sometimes the fine coal gets "caked up" and the deckhand has to go down in the cargo hold and break it loose.
(SS J.Burton Ayers 1975)

Some crew members enjoy a beautiful sunset while relaxing on deck after a full day of work. Another crew will work the night shift to keep the ship running. The ship runs twenty-four hours a day. Seven days a week. (SS J. Burton Ayers summer 1975)

The mail boat J.W. Wescott comes alongside the ship in the Detroit river and the deck crew lower a pail with the outgoing mail and provides the incoming mail and newspapers. The ship doesn't stop, it only slows down during this hand-off. (SS J. Burton Ayers 1975)

(SS J. Burton Ayers 1975)

A view up the deck of the SS J. Burton Ayers. The unloading boom swings out over the dock to discharge its cargo on the dock. (1975)

A beautiful sunny day on Lake Huron, summer of 1975. (SS J. Burton Ayers)

The M/V Columbia Star is one of several thousand Footers on the Great Lakes.

The Columbia star was built in Sturgeon Bay Wisconsin at the Bay Shipbuilding Company in 1981. In 2003 myself and another Coast Guard officer Rode the Columbia star from Toledo to Duluth Minnesota, picked up a load of iron ore and back to Toledo. We were observing the company's operating procedures. (2003, upbound)

Once the ship is in the lock the gates close behind it before lowering the vessel down to the level of the lower St. Mary's river

After the ship passes through the Soo locks it proceeds down the St. Mary's River. It takes about 5 hours to navigate all the way down the river to Lake Huron. (M/V Columbia Star 2003)

The lower gates close after the ship pulls out of the lock to get ready for the next down bound ship

(M/V Columbia Star 2003)

(M/V Columbia Star, 2003 down bound)

This is a view from the bridge on the motor vessel Columbia Star, the thousand-foot ship. This is where the captain sits when he watches over the boat and navigates across the lake.

(M/V Columbia Star 2003)

The Great Lakes are usually calm during the summer but wait until November that's when the big storms come. They call them the "Gales of November".

A view up the deck to the forward end

Looking up at the bridge from the main spar deck,
The after cabin is about five stories tall

It's a long walk from one end of the ship to the other. (M/V Columbia Star, 2003)

A crew member changes a light bulb in the navigation lights high above the vessel

A Canadian freighter we passed on Lake Superior as we were upbound to Duluth Minnesota.

These ships are now equipped with the latest navigation equipment including satellite GPS tracking and charts. This ship is called a motor vessel, MV for short because it is powered by two huge diesel engines. Some of the older ships like the ones I sailed on have steam turbine engines in them and they have two big boilers that heat the water and make the steam. Those ships are called steamships instead of motor vessel. (M/V Oglebay Norton, 2003)

My Buddy, Bernie Tufts from the Coast Guard office in Toledo. A great guy to work with. (M/V Oglebay Norton, 2003)

This is a steam turbine in the engine room of one of the ships that I sailed on in 1973 and 1974. The name of this ship was the SS Armco. The steam from the boilers shoots through nozzles and turns a high-speed turbine made by Westinghouse. The main generators were also steam turbine with a diesel-powered backup generator.

This is a picture of me working in the engine room on the SS Middletown in 1976. Keeping an eye on all the gauges and temperatures in the engine room was just part of my job. I was 22 years old.

The stainless-steel kitchen or "Galley" as it is called on a ship. This is where the cook works, and he prepares all the meals for the entire crew 3 times a day. (SS Armco, 1974)

The SS Middletown, it was a steamship and it was the best job I ever had. The Middletown was built in 1943 and it used to be an ocean-going tanker for Gulf oil. After it had a fire onboard, they gutted the tanker and turn it into a bulk carrier and brought it up to the Great Lakes. Because it used to be an ocean-going vessel it was one of the fastest ships on the Great Lakes. (Photographer unknown)

During the winter months when the Great Lakes are all Frozen, the ships layup for the whole entire winter, some of them have to go into the Dry Dock at the shipyard every 5 years for an inspection. This is a ship that was in the Toledo Shipyard Dry Dock for inspection. This is the actual bottom of the ship called the SS Reserve. This is one of the many ships that I inspected when I was at the Coast Guard Office in Toledo. (Winter, 2003)

The huge bronze propeller that powers the ship and the rudder that steers it must also be inspected when it's in the dry dock at the shipyard. (SS Reserve, winter 2003)

Sailing on the Great Lakes during the summertime gives you the chance to see some of the most beautiful sunsets. There is nothing more peaceful than sitting out on deck in the evening watching the sun go down.

(M/V Oglebay Norton 2003)

Sunset from the deck of the Columbia Star on Lake Superior, It's July but the air temperature is 43 degrees and the water temperature is 39 degrees

The hot sun sinks into Lake Superior,
but it never warms the water

Timothy

Almost gone

Timothy

The sky looks like fire after sunset on Lake Superior, Absolute Tranquility!

A few minutes after sunset the moon rises over the Keweenaw Peninsula on the shore of Lake Superior

The moon lights up the lake like a giant streetlight.

(photographer unknown)

The Gales of November

During the wintertime, especially the month of November, it is a completely different situation on the Lakes when the storms move in. The Gales of November as they call them, bring ferocious storms to the Great Lakes with very rough weather and high seas.
The witch of November, or November witch, refers to the strong winds that frequently blow across the Great Lakes in autumn. The witches are caused by intense low atmospheric pressure over the Great Lakes pulling cold Canadian Arctic air from the North or Northwest and warm gulf air from the south. When these cold and warm air masses collide, they can result it hurricane-force winds that stir up large waves on the Lakes.

SS Edmund Fitzgerald was an American Great Lakes freighter that sank in a Lake Superior storm on November 10, 1975, with the loss of the entire crew of 29. When launched on June 7, 1958, she was the largest ship on North America's Great Lakes, and she remains the largest to have sunk there.
The SS Edmund Fitzgerald was 728 feet long and the largest ship to sink on the Great Lakes.

(photographer unknown)

This is a ship during the month of November in a storm. The waves wash over the deck completely and the hatch covers must be secured to keep the ship from sinking.

(photographer unknown)

The SS Middletown that I sailed on and took this picture the next day after the storm was over, everything was covered with ice.

The SS Armco coming in off of Lake Huron into the St. Clair River after a bad storm, everything is covered with ice. The waves would freeze as soon as they hit the ship and the deck. (Photographer Ken Hamilton)

A Great Lakes freighter during a storm on Lake Superior.
(Photographer unknown)

On the night of November 10th, 1975, a ferocious storm swept across the Great Lakes. We were on Lake Huron at the time of the storm, and at 7:10 p.m. that night the Edmund Fitzgerald disappeared on Lake Superior with all her 29 crew members. When we finally got to the North end of Lake Huron, we anchored in the Mackinac straits to take shelter from The Storm. The next day we went up the St. Mary's River and through the Soo locks to go out onto Lake Superior.

When we went through the Soo locks the next day, someone in Sault Ste Marie Michigan gave us a wreath for the memory of the ship. when we got to the area of where the ship sank, the captain circled the area possibly looking for any survivors that might have been in the water, none were found. A lot of debris was found by the coast guard and other ships searching the area such as an oil slick, life jackets, life rings, and other floating objects.

As we circled over the area where the ship was lying on the bottom of the lake, the entire crew assembled on deck to hold a memorial service. Many of us on the ship knew some of the fellas on the Fitzgerald, we had sailed with them in previous years on other vessels. The captain of our vessel, Delmar Webster dropped the wreath in the water over the area where the Fitzgerald sank.

It was a very somber time for all the crew members and me as we circled the site where the Fitzgerald was lost. The freighter Edmund Fitzgerald was 728 ft. long and carrying a cargo of 26 thousand tons of iron ore.

The crew on my ship assemble on deck for a small memorial service for the crew of the Edmund Fitzgerald as we circle the location of the sinking. (SS J. Burton Ayers 1975)

Captain Delmar Webster dropping the wreath in the cold waters of Lake Superior to honor our fellow shipmates who were lost the night before. this event was less than 24 hours after the Fitzgerald sank.

The investigation that followed by the U.S. Coast Guard and the National Transportation Safety board never reached an absolute conclusion as to the reason why the vessel was lost.

As of this writing in 2019, there has not been another shipwreck on the Great Lakes since the SS Edmund Fitzgerald.

Rogue wave theory

A group of three rogue waves, often called "three sisters," was reported in the vicinity of Edmund Fitzgerald at the time she sank. The "three sisters" phenomenon is said to occur on Lake Superior as a result of a sequence of three rogue waves forming that are one-third larger than normal waves. The first wave introduces an abnormally large amount of water onto the deck. This water is unable to fully drain away before the second wave strikes, adding to the surplus. The third incoming wave again adds to the two accumulated backwashes, quickly overloading the deck with too much water.

A ship owned by U.S. Steel, The SS Arthur M. Anderson, was following the Fitzgerald and tracking her on radar. The Fitzgerald had lost her radar antennas from above the bridge due to waves and wind and the captain, Jesse Cooper was helping the Fitzgerald navigate by radio.

Captain Cooper of Arthur M. Anderson reported that his ship was "hit by two 30 to 35-foot seas about 6:30 p.m., one burying the aft cabins and damaging a lifeboat by pushing it right down onto the saddle. The second wave of this size, perhaps 35 foot, came over the bridge deck." Cooper went on to say that these two waves, possibly followed by a third, continued in the direction of Edmund Fitzgerald and would have struck about the time she sank. This theory postulates that the "three sisters" compounded the twin problems of Edmund Fitzgerald's known list and her lower speed in heavy seas that already allowed water to remain on her deck for longer than usual.

By late in the afternoon of November 10, sustained winds of over 50 knots (58 mph) were recorded by ships and observation points across eastern Lake Superior. Arthur M. Anderson logged sustained winds as high as 58 knots (67 mph) at 4:52 p.m., while waves increased to as high as 25 feet by 6:00 p.m. Arthur M. Anderson was also struck by 70-to-75-knot (81 to 86 mph) gusts and rogue waves as high as 35 feet.

The last communication from the ship came at approximately 7:10 p.m., when Arthur M. Anderson notified Edmund Fitzgerald of an upbound ship and asked how she was doing. Captain McSorley reported, "We are holding our own." She sank minutes later. No distress signal was received, and ten minutes later, Arthur M. Anderson lost the ability either to raise Edmund Fitzgerald by radio or to detect her on radar.

(source Wikipedia)

it's this author's opinion that the Fitzgerald did bottom out on the six fathom Shoals. Captain Cooper testified in the investigation that he thought the Edmund Fitzgerald was too close to the Shoals. That would have ruptured the hull of the ship allowing water to enter the vessel. The captain knew he had water in his ship and the engine room was trying to pump it out as fast as they could. The added weight of the water on top of 26,000 tons of cargo caused the vessel to nosedive all the way to the bottom of the Lake when they were hit with a massive following sea.

These are the crewmembers of the SS Edmund Fitzgerald lost at sea November 10, 1975

Michael E. Armagost
37
Third Mate
Iron River, Wisconsin

Fred J. Beetcher
56
Porter
Superior, Wisconsin

Thomas D. Bentsen
23
Oiler
St. Joseph, Michigan

Edward F. Bindon
47
First Asst. Engineer
Fairport Harbor, Ohio

Thomas D. Borgeson
41
Maintenance Man
Duluth, Minnesota

Oliver J. Champeau
41
Third Asst. Engineer
Sturgeon Bay, Wisconsin

Nolan S. Church
55
Porter
Silver Bay, Minnesota

Ransom E. Cundy
53
Watchman
Superior, Wisconsin

These are the crewmembers of the SS Edmund Fitzgerald lost at sea November 10, 1975 (cont'd)

Thomas E. Edwards
50
Second Asst. Engineer
Oregon, Ohio

Russell G. Haskell
40
Second Asst. Engineer
Millbury, Ohio

George J. Holl
60
Chief Engineer
Cabot, Pennsylvania

Bruce L. Hudson
22
Deck Hand
North Olmsted, Ohio

Allen G. Kalmon
43
Second Cook
Washburn, Wisconsin

Gordon F. MacLellan
30
Wiper
Clearwater, Florida

Joseph W. Mazes
59
Special Maintenance Man
Ashland, Wisconsin

John H. McCarthy
62
First Mate
Bay Village, Ohio

These are the crewmembers of the SS Edmund Fitzgerald lost at sea November 10, 1975 (cont'd)

Ernest M. McSorley
63
Captain
Toledo, Ohio

Eugene W. O'Brien
50
Wheelsman
Toledo, Ohio

Karl A. Peckol
20
Watchman
Ashtabula, Ohio

John J. Poviach
59
Wheelsman
Bradenton, Florida

James A. Pratt
44
Second Mate
Lakewood, Ohio

Robert C. Rafferty
62
Steward
Toledo, Ohio

Paul M. Riippa
22
Deck Hand
Ashtabula, Ohio

These are the crewmembers of the SS Edmund Fitzgerald lost at sea November 10, 1975 (cont'd)

John D. Simmons
63
Wheelsman
Ashland, Wisconsin

William J. Spengler
59
Watchman
Toledo, Ohio

Mark A. Thomas
21
Deck Hand
Richmond Heights, Ohio

Ralph G. Walton
58
Oiler
Fremont, Ohio

David E. Weiss
22
Cadet
Agoura, California

Blaine H. Wilhelm
52
Oiler
Moquah, Wisconsin

(source Wikipedia)

THE END!

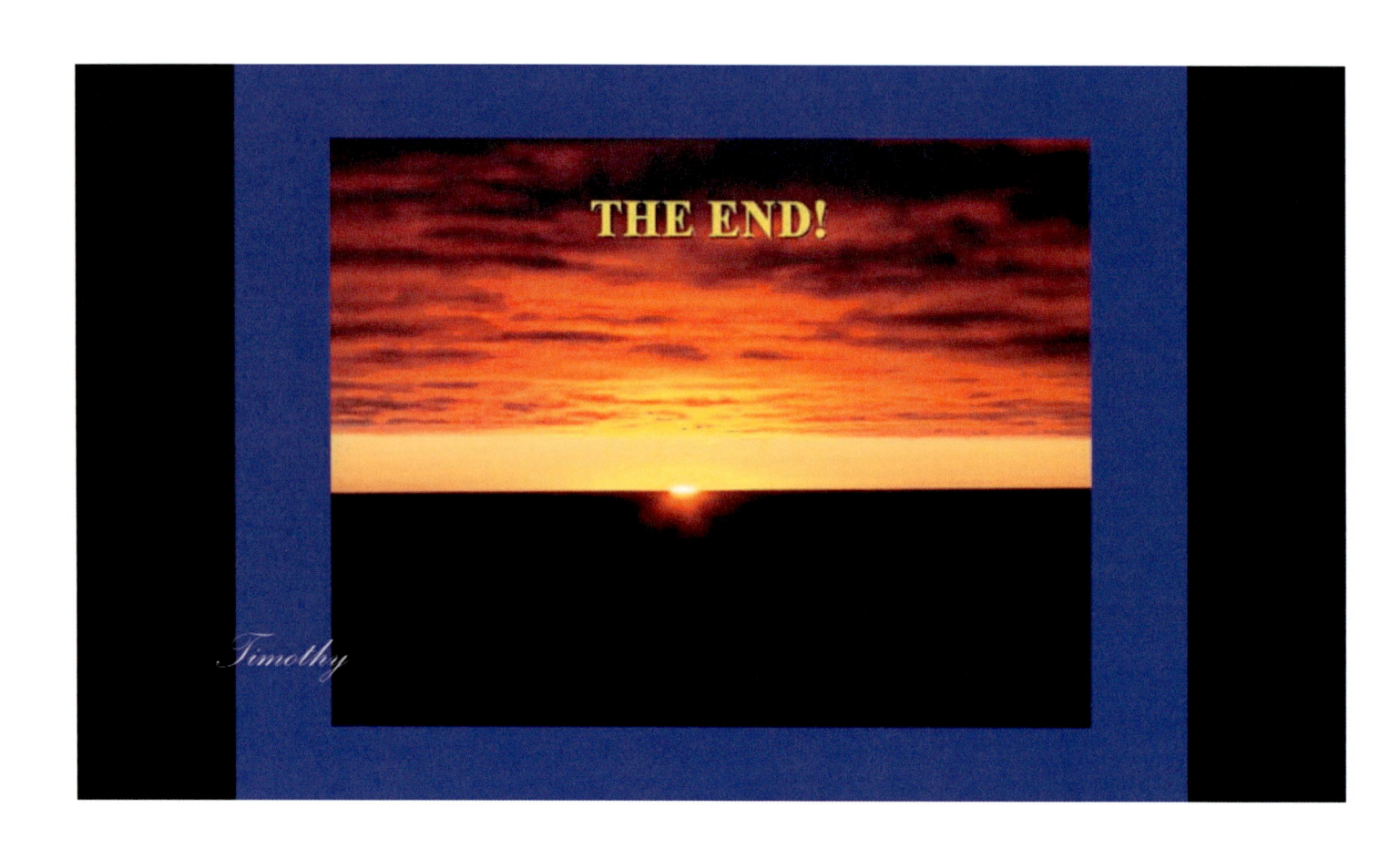

Timothy